Acknowledgements

This book has been so much fun to write and compile. My friends have been so wonderful in giving me their support, encouragement and ideas. I especially want to thank Sue Conklin, Nancy Knuth, Phyllis Yeager, and our daughter, Pam Barnard for their undying encouragement. I also want to thank members of my Book Club who took the time to jot down their ideas on this tedious subject. Without these people, I never could have completed this work.

I

I have collected quotes since I was fifteen. I do have some original quotes but most of these I've collected over the years. I have tried to give proper credit when I have known who was directly responsible.

I sincerely thank all the clever people who have made these quotes possible! Happy reading and peace to you!

Pricilla Perfect

Oh, I wish
I could be a
Mother-In-Law
like this . . .

By Pricilla Perfect

*Wise, Witty and Wonderfully Practical
Advice For Mothers-In-Law*

Cover Design, Art & Typesetting by
Marta Shattuck Romansky

ISBN:0-9615622-6-9

Table of Contents

Life may not be fair, but mothers-in-law can be.

This book is dedicated in loving memory to my mother Birdie Lee Brown Warnock and to my mother-in-law Augusta Claire Castellaw McElyea, who were the world's greatest mothers-in-law.

Point-of-View

*The following story was told to me shortly after
I became a mother-in-law.*

Two women who had not seen each other in a long time met by chance in the supermarket. One said to the other, "I hear you had a daughter and a son marry over the summer. How do you like your new son-in-law?"

The other woman answered,
"Oh, he's a wonderful young man. He mops the kitchen floor for her. He goes to the grocery store with her. He takes out the garbage and he even loads the dishwasher. He's just a great addition to the family!"

The first woman replied,
"Well isn't that nice. And how do you
like your new daughter-in-law?"
The woman answered,
"Oh, she's the laziest thing you've ever
seen! My poor son has to mop the
kitchen floor, go to the grocery, take

out the garbage, and he even has to load the dishwasher for her. She's a real lazy girl!"

. . . Just depends on your point-of-view!

Smiles increase your face value.

We have a perfect son-in-law and two perfect daughters-in-law. They are perfect because they make our children happy. One ought not ask for more than this.

Preface

In gathering material for this book, I talked with women from many walks of life. Most of their concerns were the same as yours and mine -- It's not Shakespeare's

"To be or not to be." Rather it's the mother-in-law's confused cry,

"HOW TO BE!"

Smiles and good humor are the seasoning that make everything living taste better.

Chapter 1

Secrets of Being The Perfect Mother-In-Law

"It has been my experience that folks who have no vices have very few virtues."

Abraham Lincoln

Treat your new daughter-in-law or son-in-law like a friend you are trying to win over. Love them as you love your children, but *give advice carefully and sparingly.*

Don't nurse a grudge.

A friend told me that being
a mother-in-law was the biggest
challenge she'd had since the birth
of her first child. Just remember that
a new challenge is always rewarding
if you give it all you've got!

Forty is the old age of youth; fifty
is the youth of old age.   Victor Hugo

Thank your son-in-law and daughter-in-law for the nice things they do for your child. Their short-comings will fade. "Love does not keep a record of wrongs."
I Corinthians 13:5c

Laughter is a tranquilizer with no side effects!

Make sure their privacy
is very, very important
to you.

A fool thinks he needs no advice,
but a wise man listens to others.

Proverbs 12:15

Make at least one flower
arrangement for them when
they are entertaining (even
if you have to buy it!)

Make sure when giving a party that you
are not the most interesting person there.

*Offer to make their favorite dessert
when they're having a party!!*

*Sometimes people mistake
endurance for hospitality!*

Remember their way of doing something really might be better than your way!!!

Some people are very bossy, but they boss with a smile!!

Find a common ground you can
both laugh about, or talk about.
Let them lead. It just might open
up some pretty interesting topics!

Do your best and angels can do no more.

One mother-in-law made a rule that her newly married children had to live at least a day's drive from their hometown the first year.

Be a good listener. If your son-in-law or daughter-in-law complains about their mate's imperfections, just listen patiently. Don't agree or disagree. Whatever you do, don't admit to knowing their faults. And don't say that, if you could have, you already would have corrected them. This way you won't get into a disagreement.

Behind every successful man there is a mother-in-law that made it necessary!!

Don't hog the holidays. I know it's hard and that you hate to miss your grandchild's first Christmas or Channukah. But send them off with love and Godspeed. If it's a gift sharing holiday, be sure and send something for the "other" in-laws.

Here's a little something for you to think about . . .We, alone are responsible for our happiness.

Don't live your life through your children. Get involved in activities that you really enjoy. Treat yourself. Be happy. This is the best way to make your children happy. They'll have lots to tell you when you all get together, and you'll have lots to tell them! This is what goes into the making of a truly happy family. Let your

children go, and they'll return
with arms full of love.

*Family jokes are the bond that keep
families alive.*
                    Stella Benson
                    1892-1933

Think often of the proverb,

"A Soft Tongue Can Break Hard Bones".

A mother-in-law's tongue should
be sweet and savvy in order
to keep her children-in-laws happy.

A little sugar never hurt a lemon . . .

Never, never, never, ever talk about one daughter or son-in-law to another!

If you are heading in the wrong direction, God allows U-turns.

Work hard at making your children and their spouses feel your wholehearted support and approval. We cannot, even though we would like to, keep them from making mistakes. They have to make and correct their own mistakes. Just be there with support and sympathy, when they realize what they should have done. Don't say "I told you so. . ."

A word of encouragement during failure is worth more than a dictionary of praise after success.

Share some of your mistakes - if
the opportunity presents itself -
as well as some of your solutions.

Work is love made visible.
                    Kahil Gibran

Don't wear your feelings on your sleeve. Put on a hard shell, like a turtle. Smile and swallow any slights you might feel, and affirm to yourself they were unintentional. Isn't this what we taught our children to do?

Diplomacy is thinking twice before saying nothing.

If something is better left unsaid, leave it there.

Be kind to each other, tenderhearted, forgiving one another. *Ephesians 4:32*

Hold out a helping hand rather than point a critical finger.

Don't ever remind them if it wasn't for you they wouldn't have their mate - they might want revenge!!!

Some people wade through life; others pan for gold.

Make lots of happy memories.
There's no substitute for them.

Good character-like good soup-
is usually homemade.

Take lots of pictures of your children, and always have copies made for them.

A reiteration: Don't depend on your children for your happiness. Stay involved in your own activities-career, politics, church, bridge, charity work. Any hobby that you really love makes you a more interesting person.

Think happy thoughts. Whenever an unhappy thought pops into your head, replace it with something good that someone has said about you OR something that you've done to bring happiness to another person.

Don't talk about yourself.
Others will do that for you.

*Be free with your compliments
and stingy with your criticism.*

*Approval is the key to winning a son-in-law
or a daughter-in-law's love.*

A beautiful diamond doesn't just happen. It takes someone to recognize it's value and polish it up. If one of your children marries someone you're initially not that fond of, give them

a little time and some kind attention.
It just might be they're a diamond
in the rough.

Buy your children and their spouses things they can't afford for themselves. Don't worry about leaving them an inheritance. Give now and watch them enjoy things they want and need. Do only what you can afford to do.

Pray everyday for wisdom and patience.

Character is a by-product; it is produced
in the great manufacture of daily duty.
Woodrow Wilson

When you give your children gifts,
do it with a full heart, open arms
and no strings.

Keep your mouth shut and your head a noddin"!!!

One gift your children can always use is money. But if you help them financially, let them decide how to spend it.

If you have the urge to meddle in your children's lives once they've married, find another hobby.

Be a volunteer baby sitter. This is a wonderful time to bond with your grandchildren.

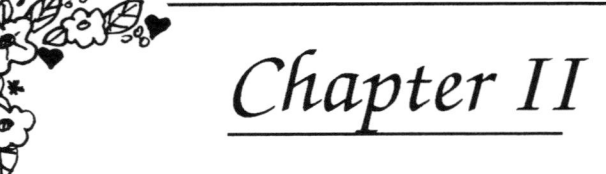

Chapter II

Perfect Grandchildren and Perfect Mothers-In-Law

Always make sure the grandchildren have special fun times when visiting you. Read to them. Take them to the park, the zoo, a movie. Bake cookies. Paint their fingernails. Do things that they don't get to do at home. Take them to the Mall and ride the escalator with them- 15 mos. to 2 1/2 yrs. love this!!

Love is spelled T-I-M-E to a child.

Forgive your grandchildren's mistakes. Think back to when you were young. It takes a long time and a lot of mistakes to get as wise as we are now.

Tell your children and their spouses how much you love your grandchildren and how exceptionally bright and beautiful they are - and besides being bright and beautiful, they are also perfect!!! Their mom and dad are doing a great job when it comes to child raising.

Treat your grandchildren equally.
Use the same rules for all the
youngsters, because they quickly
sense favoritism. Remember, little
egos are very fragile.

A child is a curly, dimpled lunatic.
Ralph Waldo Emerson
1803-1882

Chapter III

How Not To Be A Boring Mother-In-Law

If you have a special hide-away (beach house, mountain cabin, condo, etc.) have a key made for your children. Tell them to call to arrange the date they'd like. Make them feel they are free to use it with or without you. They might want to take friends or a special business client.

Take them on family vacations-
EVEN if it pinches the pocketbook!

Buy your grandchild a "just because
I'm sick present" when he's sick.

When the children and/or
grandchildren come to visit, have
a jigsaw puzzle on the game table.
Begin to work it and, before you
know it, they'll be joining you.

Have themed dinner parties. For instance, Mexican, Italian, Spanish, English, German, etc. Carry out the theme by coordinating the *cuisine, table decorations, music, and maybe even after-dinner games around the concept of your special country.*

Tell them to bring over their photographs, and serve a simple one-dish meal. Then work on the photo albums after dinner.

It's a good way for everybody to get their albums caught up. This is a warm, wonderful way to promote family conviviality.

Stay informed as to what's happening in the world. Be an interesting guest because, after your spouse, your children are the most important people in your life and the ones you love the most. They should always be treated that way and never taken for granted. They are special and should be made to feel that way.

Chapter IV

Tips For Sons-In-Law and Daughters-In-Law

Praise your mate extravagantly and don't point out any shortcomings. After all, your mother-in-law brought them up and already knows their strengths, as well as their weaknesses!

Call your mother-in-law "Mom",
"Mother", or by her given name.

Include your In-laws at some of your couples parties.

Speak well of your mother-in-law
to your parents and to your friends.
If she has some idiosyncracies,
share them with your mate only!!!

Go to your house of worship together. You'll find some of the best people there.

Tell your mother-in-law, "Let's go to lunch (or to the movies, an art show, etc.). Invite your mate's parents for dinner once every two or three months- at least.

Close your eyes to the faults of others and watch the doors of friendship swing wide open.

When you have family get-togethers, include the brother or sister or other relative you are not wild about! The family will love and respect you for this.

Real difficulties can be overcome; it is only the imaginary ones that are unconquerable.

Tell your mother-in-laws' friends how great she is. This will really make her feel good - you can bet it will get back to her.

It is possible for one to tell you all the facts and still not all the truth.

Don't pout when things don't go exactly as you'd like. Your mother-in-law might like things to be different too!!

Don't treat your mother-in-law like she has one foot in the grave and the other on a banana peel. Everybody likes to think of themselves as younger than they really are!

The people we remember after they are gone are the people who remembered us while they wre alive.

Treat your mate the way you want your children's mate to treat them.

The heart that loves is always young.
> Favorite quote of
> Jeanne Gillitte
> Watertown, NY

Always make sure your mate isn't hungry when you have a controversial issue to discuss. People, all of us, are more pleasant, receptive, and easy going when our stomachs are full.

This smart strategy is also called "Waiting for the right moment!"

Don't turn the light out on your grievances. Grievances, like rabbits, multiply in the dark.

It takes both rain and sunshine to make a rainbow.

Favorite quote of
Jeanne Gillitte
Watertown, NY

Accept your mother-in-law, bumps and all. Sometimes bumps turn out to be beautiful muscles of strength.

The young sow wild oats; the old grow sage.

Favorite quote of
Jeanne Gillitte
Watertown, NY

Try not to take all of your
mother-in-law's espousings too
seriously . . . she probably doesn't.

A clear conscience is the sign of a
bad memory.

Favorite quote of
Jeanne Gillitte
Watertown, NY

Chapter V

Family Trips-
Get Your Pocketbooks
Open. . .WIDE!

A trip to the Big Apple, New York City, can be a special delight for each member of your family.

We took our children and grand-children on this trip at Christmastime. With the decorations, crisp weather, and special holiday events, it was one of the most exciting vacations we've ever taken.

95

*Get your travel agent to plan this
one for you to suit your special
interests and budget. We went
separate ways many days, and
then met for dinner to share what
we'd done during the day. We*

stayed eight days and each one was jam-packed! The trip is a memory we will always have with us.

(Travel agents get their commissions from the airlines and hotels. There is no charge to you for their services.)

Take a snow skiing trip. Check with
a travel agent to schedule your
vacation when the area normally has
the best ski conditions.

Many an optimist has become rich by
buying out a pessimist.

Try a week in the Blue Ridge Mountains in the summer. It's nice and cool for golf, tennis, mountain climbing, panning for rubies, and picnics.

Plan a trip to New England to see the Autumn colors. But plan a year in advance. Those quaint bed and breakfasts are popular and fill up early.

If you love someone you will be loyal to him no matter what the cost.
I Corinthians 13:7a

Try a week at the beach for
a variety of sun-filled activities.
Have special T-shirts made
featuring beach week, a special
anniversary, birthday, etc.

Take lots of games, and don't forget the volleyball. Make sand candles (if you can't find the instructions for these at the library, send me a SASE.) There are so many things to do at the beach, like flying a kite, floating on the waves, *walking along the water's edge at sunset, even helping your grand-children find the perfect shell or shark's tooth. The secret of a wonderful beach vacation is to have activities planned, while*

you also allow for free time.
And don't forget the burgers and
dogs easy barbecue dinners.
They're almost required fare.

*Ideas are funny little things. They won't
work unless you do.*

Go on a cruise together. Everything is planned. You just have to pick and choose what you like the best.

Neurotics build castles in the sky. Psychotics live in them. Psychiatrists collect the rent.

Why not try a trip to a multi-purpose resort. They usually have baby sitting for toddlers as well as golf, tennis, horseback riding, bicycling trails, fishing, bridge, and many other activities.

Lazy: Whittling with an electric knife!

Chapter VI

Gatherings of The Clan

Teach your children by example-
By example- By example-
Only!!!

Teach them to plan ahead for the things that need to be done before a party, family dinner, any kind of gathering, whether large or small.

For example, teach them that when
you're having company you've got
to plan the food preparation,
secure baby sitters (sometimes a
week or more ahead of time),
polish silver, decide on decorations

and entertainment. You've even got to plan the house cleaning, both inside and outside, before entertaining. Never wait until the day before an occasion to begin preparation for it's success.

Whether you're running the party or just a guest, the best thing you can wear is a smile. Wrap yourself in patience and remember that every family has a few eccentrics, and that's what makes it special.

It's impossible to mend a fence if you are sitting on it.

Find the humor in the situation.
Whether your depression- era
mother-in-law is wrapping the
restaurant's dinner rolls in paper
napkins and stashing them in

her purse, or your daughter-in-law's place cards have you sitting at the children's table for the third year in a row, think positive thoughts and enjoy yourself. Make your corner of the world a

Vows made in storms are forgotten in calms.

special place. Each little annoyance can be spun into a humorous story when you re-tell it later on.

Remember In-laws have a compulsion to turn off lights. My father-in-law used to actually follow me around turning off lights after me!. . . But he loved me even with my warts!!

Try to entertain your children's spouses equally over the course of the year. Inviting the cherished daughter-in-law for dinner at your private club, and the other

*for take-out, won't create harmony
or leave your children a legacy of
love and respect.*

Life isn't fair but mothers-in-law can be!

Chapter VII

Mother-In-Law Cake

Mother-In-Law Cake

Preheat oven to 350°

Grease two 9" round
cake pans

1 stick butter-softened
2 cups sugar
3 large eggs
1 tsp. vanilla

2 cups self-rising flour
2 tbsp. cocoa
2 tbsp. cinnamon
1 cup buttermilk

Mix together, using electric mixer, butter, sugar and
eggs. Beat until light and fluffy. Add alternately the
flour, cocoa and cinnamon with the buttermilk.

119

Mix on medium speed for 2 minutes. Pour into well greased cake pans and bake for 30 - 35 minutes or until cake tester or a broom straw or toothpick comes out clean when inserted in cake layers. Let cool and then turn out onto wax paper before frosting.

Frosting

1/3 cup butter or
  margarine
1 cup firmly packed
  brown sugar
1/8 tsp. salt

1/4 cup milk
1/2 tsp. vanilla
1 1/2 cups Ten X
  confectioners sugar
  (sifted)

Melt butter in saucepan; add brown sugar and cook over low heat for 2 minutes, stirring constantly. Add salt and milk and continue stirring until mixture comes to a boil. Boil 3 minutes; remove from heat and cool. Add vanilla; blend well. Gradually beat in confectioners sugar and continue beating until mixture is smooth and of spreading consistency. Frost bottom layer when cool. Place second layer on top of first layer and frost - bringing icing down the sides.

From my cousin, Jeannine B. Browning's cookbook, _Sand In My Shoes_.

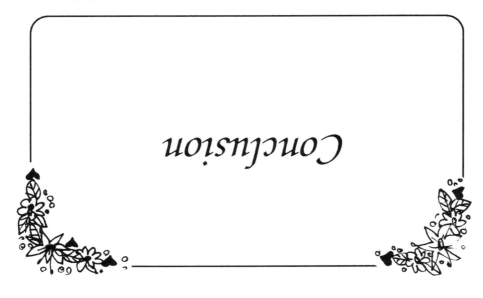

Conclusion

Conclusion

Being a mother-in-law is probably the toughest role in the world. You have to be a mediator, a mentor, a mother, and always a diplomat. Just take solace in the knowledge that, if she plays her cards as well

as you have, your daughter-in-law
will someday be a mother-in-law
as wonderful as you!

If you have something you would like to add to this book, please be so kind as to send it to me.
I am interested in funny mother-in-law, daughter-in-law and son-in-law stories. - - - Or in-law stories in general.

If we use your material, we will give you credit and give you the revised edition.

Thanks and God Bless!

Chapter IX

In-Law Stories

Visiting some quaint handicrafts shops while on vacation, the young couple was looking for a small gift for husband's mother. After careful deliberation, the daughter-in-law selected a straw broom, which she thought would look attractive on her mother-in-law's front door. Upon presentation of the gift, the daughter-in-law said, "You might just want to ride it home!" Stunned, the mother-in-law's mouth fell open.

"Oh, that's all right, Mom," her son smiled. "She's already broken it in!"

The mother-in-law paid an overnight visit to her son and his family who lived a few towns away. While in the house, she complained about the way the house was run, especially the request that people not smoke inside. When the visit *was over and she was preparing to leave, she admonished her DAUGHTER-IN-LAW for having rules that did not make her feel like a welcomed guest.*

A few months later, the mother-in-law, her son and his family were invited to her DAUGHTER'S home for dinner. All evening long, whenever the children disagreed, or a procedure or custom had to be followed, the DAUGHTER'S rules prevailed. When a disagreement ensued, the mother-in-law snapped, "It's her house and she gets to set the rules!"

Exasperated, the DAUGHTER-IN-LAW asked, "When do I get to set the rules?"

One mother-in-law told me if she could buy her daughter's mother-in-law for what she was worth and could sell her for what she THOUGHT she was worth, she would be worth millions!

Another mother-in-law, who has a wonderful relationship with her daughter-in-law, said that when her son was first married if he was ten minutes late getting home, the new little daughter-in-law was on the phone calling her to see if he had stopped by to see his mother. She said she would say "No, I haven't seen him," as she would be shoving him out the door!!! The daughter-in-law and the mother-in-law now laugh about this scenerio!!!

Happy memories shared with a loved one become keepsakes in your mind.

The average family's ambition is to make as much money as they're spending!

Consider how hard it is to change yourself and you'll understand what little chance you have of trying to change others.

Jacob M. Braude

Other books published by
McElyea Publications:

Sweet Surrender
with advice a la-carte
(A cookbook of sweets)

Advice Southern Style

A Toast To You

Just Between You and Me

Pet Repair

Toast of the Town